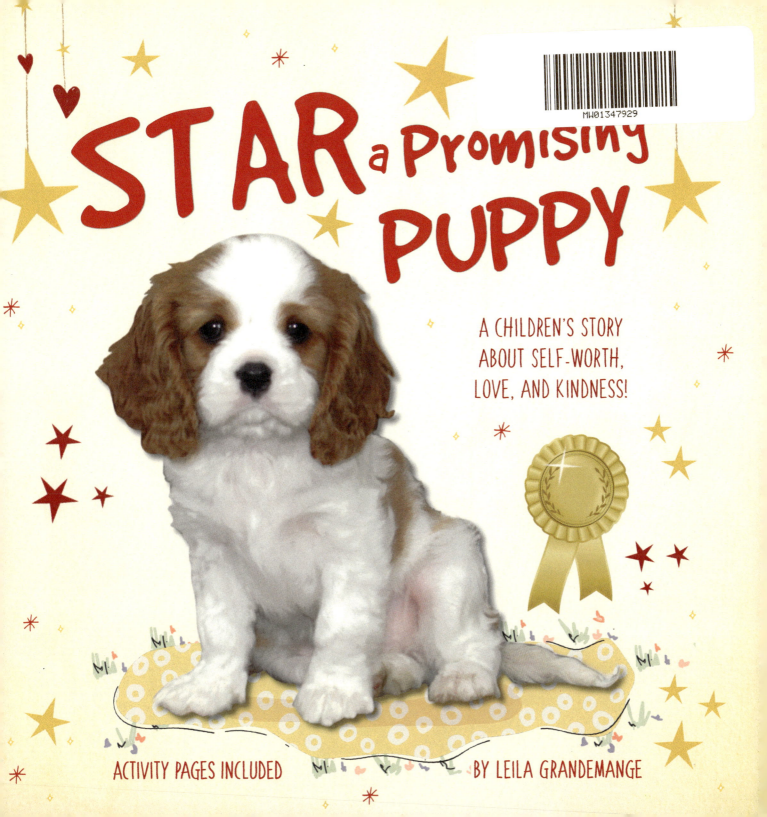

Star, A Promising Puppy

A Children's Story about Self-Worth, Love, and Kindness.
Activity Pages for Kids and Positive Affirmations Included!

Copyright © 2020 by Leila Grandemange
www.LeilaGrandemange.com

ISBN: 978-0-9975658-4-3

All rights reserved. No part of this publication may be reproduced, stored in a retrieval system, or transmitted in any form or by any means electronic, mechanical, photocopy, recording, or any other except in the case of brief quotations embodied in critical articles or reviews, without prior permission of the publisher.

Credits

Cover and interior design by Leila Grandemange.

Image Credits:

All dogs photographed are Grandville Cavaliers, by Leila Grandemange.

Assistance with photography:
Jeremie Grandemange, pages 30,32
Christy Jones, pages 8,39
Nichols Photography, pages 40,41

Design elements courtesy of Istockphoto and Shutterstock.
Cover: Yellow blanket and grass elements by Lisa Glanz.

Editing, ED&M Design, Virginia

SunnyVille Publishing

This book is lovingly dedicated to you,

A Shining Star!

May you discover how bright and beautiful you truly are!

Once upon a time on a morning so chilly,
I was born a wee pup to a dog breeder named Billy.

I'm a Cavalier King Charles, "Star" is my name,
Short for "Bright Shining Star"—a show name with fame!

Told I was promising, that my future was bright,
He cared for me and loved me with all of his might!

I felt really special, beautiful, and smart,
My heart was happy, so I let out a bark.

He had a large mirror, so fancy and old,
Before it I sat, my face to behold.

"Tell me old Mirror, what do you see?"
The Mirror reflected these words just for me . . .

I see joyful love aglow in your heart, radiant fur, a bright work of art. Head held so high, set on a throne, sparkling eyes and shimmers of gold. Movement so graceful, a dancer by far, surely you are A PROMISING STAR!

Beholding my beauty, this image so sweet,
Joy filled my being as I leaped to my feet!
Spinning in circles, I jumped to the sky,
I chased after balls, I felt I could fly.

With Billy I ran, I played all the days,
The things that he taught me were all filled with praise.
To obey was a game, I loved chasing sticks,
I learned very quickly, especially tricks!

A sad day came; it was now time to go,
A new owner named Tom I must now get to know.

Billy said I'd be happy, they wanted a star,
A promising puppy that would surely go far.

So with hugs and a lick we said our goodbye,
Then one final word Billy spoke with pride:

"Some jewels of wisdom I really must share,
I've molded and taught him with the utmost care.

"I was the potter, he was the clay—
Continue to mold him, I trust and I pray.

"Let love and patience guide you each hour,
Then watch as he blossoms, a beautiful flower.

"Heed my advice, he'll grow into a star,
But don't leave out love, or he'll never go far."

Tom tried to listen but left in a hurry,
Dreaming of glory with his newfound puppy!

Tom seemed nice, and he fed me well,
He brushed my coat, and loved my good smell.
But he wasn't too fond of playful hugs;
Perhaps he didn't like me, so I lay on my rug.

I tried to be chipper, as good as can be,
But each day Tom left to work around three.
Tom worked outside most all of the day,
So I sat alone with no one to play.

As puppies will do, I enjoyed a good chew,
I had my own fun tasting his shoe.
The day was too long, and though I tried to smile,
I couldn't hold my potty so I left a small pile.

Then off to my crate I drifted to sleep,
And waited for Tom, I couldn't wait to greet . . .

Joy filled my heart as I heard the door;
Running to greet Tom, I skidded on the floor.

Suddenly my heart sank, and fear gripped my spine,
As Tom's face changed, I hid just in time.

Tom began yelling something about shoes,
Then seeing my potty—that was bad news!

I got a spanking, and off to my crate.
Why did he yell? My heart seemed to ache.

FEELING UNSURE

The days dragged on slowly as Tom tried to train me.
Frustration and anger came to him quickly.

I must be a failure, I must not be pretty,
I didn't hear kind words, as I did when with Billy.

But dog shows were different, and Tom seemed so proud,
Cheering me on, hoping I'd please the crowd!

Around the ring I went, trotting with the pros,
But if I didn't win, it seemed my heart froze.

A blue ribbon win brought applause and favor,
Second place or less, I felt like a failure.

Peeking through my crate, seeing sadness in his eyes,
His hopes were all dashed, he wouldn't see the prize.

Tom grew so distant; I would never be a star,
Supposing he was right, I would never go far.

I no longer walked, I no longer played,
I just lay around, and I hoped for praise.

My tail stopped its wagging,
my fur grew so limp;
Curling my back,
now I even felt sick.

So I ran to the mirror,
asking, "What do you see?"
The Mirror reflected
sad words just for me . . .

An unhappy doggie,
No hope and no zeal,
Your eyes have no sparkle,
And life no appeal. Your fur
isn't shiny, you look a bit thin,
Your movement is slow, and
you don't want to spin. Your head
hangs low, no melody in
your tail, your growth's
almost stunted and
you seem a bit frail.

My reflection brought tears
A bad feeling inside,
I could no longer look,
And the sun seemed to hide.

Home Sweet Home

FEELING HOPEFUL

The day came so soon, Tom found me a home;
Said I'd make a good pet and I'd not be alone.
Not even a tear was brought to his eye,
As I gave him a lick and said my goodbye.

Now worried thoughts danced in my mind—
Would they even love me; would they be kind?
Then I saw their faces with smiles big and wide,
And soon all my fears began to subside.

My new family held me,
we'd laugh and we'd play.
They taught me with patience
To learn and obey.

They lavished me with kisses,
Spoiled me with toys;
As my toy basket grew,
Each day brought new joys!

Walking in the sunshine,
I held my head high,

My tail started wagging,
A sparkle in my eye!

People came to greet me,
I felt like a king,

They spoke to me sweetly,
I just wanted to sing!

HOME SWEET HOME ♡

One day Tom returned; he stopped at the door,
Stunned to see such beauty greet him from the floor.
Tom then exclaimed, "Well, this dog's for show!"
And they all were amazed that he just didn't know.

"Why, this was your puppy," my family explained.
"You gave him away; Star is his name.
We've loved him and praised him, so now you can see,
He's grown up so pretty, I'm sure you'll agree."

"A puppy can't grow on good food alone,
Love makes him shine, until he's full grown.
We must never forget the best gift of all:
It's praise and it's love, no matter how small."

Tom gave a big sigh, and drew me near,
He said he was sorry, and called me so dear.
Licking Tom's hand, I looked in his eyes,
I saw my reflection and beheld the prize!

A shiny ribbon, a trophy of gold,
I'm a WINNER each day, even when I'm old!

I ran to the mirror—could this be true?
The Mirror reflected, "BELIEVE IT, IT'S YOU!"

My good looks surprised me, I turned back to see;

But no one was there—yes, surely it's me!

A bright, shining star, with love by my side,

My new family hugged me, saying, "He is our pride!"

That night in my bed,
All warm and cuddly,
My heart full of love,
I felt sort of bubbly.

Closing my eyes,
Without a care in sight,
I felt rather special
As I said my goodnight.

And now I

SPARKLE AND SHINE

Everywhere I go!

Thanks for reading my story!

Love, ♥
Star

A Prayer from Star

Dear God,

Thank you for making me special.
Thank you for making me ME.
I love my nose, my fur and paws,
Everything is UNIQUE!

Thank you for my life,
Even when it's hard.
I know I am loved,
I know I am valuable,
I know I AM ENOUGH.

Thank you that my future is bright,
Because I know my worth.
I can sparkle and shine wherever I go,
I'M A PROMISING PUPPY—
THAT I KNOW!

A Letter to you: A Shining Star!

Star's story reminds us that everyone needs to feel loved and accepted in order to shine and grow into their full potential. The Bible tells us that love is patient and kind. Love is not jealous, boastful, or proud. It is not easily angered, and it keeps no record of being wronged. Love never gives up, never loses faith, is always hopeful, and continues strong through every circumstance. It's the love in our hearts (for ourselves, others, and our furry friends) that makes us truly beautiful. It helps us to believe in ourselves and fulfill our dreams!

Do you know how loved you really are? Life isn't always easy, but never forget that your value does not depend on what people say or think about you, or how many ribbons you win in life. You are valuable because God says so. He made you beautiful and unique, and he really, really, really loves you, no matter what! So, if you want to build your self-worth, focus your attention on how God sees you, not how anyone else sees you. And never doubt your infinite worth!

In this next section, you'll find some fun activities to help you love and care for your pets, and also to remind you how valuable and loved you really are!

I WILL GIVE THANKS TO YOU, FOR I AM AWESOMELY AND WONDERFULLY MADE.

—PSALM 139:14 NHEB

Fun Activities

Pet care And positive affirmations

What Did You Learn From the Story?

Directions: Circle the letter(s) that best answers the question. There can be more than one right answer. Invite your parent or guardian to help. The page numbers also can help you find answers.

1. Billy was a responsible dog breeder. How did he care for Star? (Pages 7, 9).
   a. He was patient and kind with Star.
   b. He played with him and taught him fun tricks.
   c. He left him alone a lot.

2. How do you know Star was happy in Billy's home? (Pages 8, 9).
   a. Star ran and played with Billy, and loved chasing balls.
   b. Star barked and whined a lot.
   c. The Mirror said that Star had shiny fur and a sparkle in his eyes.

3. What wise advice did Billy give Tom when he left with Star? (Pages 13-14).
   a. Be tough. Train him hard every day.
   b. Be patient and loving with Star.
   c. Always expect him to win!

4. Tom scolded Star for chewing his shoe and making potty in the house. What would be a better way to react?
   a. I would make sure he went out to potty more often.
   b. I would not leave him alone too long.
   c. I would punish him by putting him in his crate.

5. Why do you think Star was sad at Tom's house?
   a. He didn't have enough toys to play with.
   b. He was left alone most of the day.
   c. He didn't get a lot of love and affirmation.

6. What are some possible signs that can let you know a dog is unhappy?
   a. His tail is tucked between his legs.
   b. He doesn't want to eat or play.
   c. He might whine, bark a lot, act nervous, or chew things he shouldn't.

7. The decision to bring a puppy home is a big commitment. How did Star's new family show they were committed to Star's happiness and well-being?
   a. They were patient and kind and took time to walk Star and play with him.
   b. They crated him all day and rarely paid attention to him.
   c. They praised him often and loved him unconditionally.

8. How do we know Star was happy with his new family? (Pages 34-42).
   a. Star was wagging and walking with his new owner and greeting people.
   b. Star was playing with his toys and had a sparkle in his eyes.
   c. Star felt loved and slept well.

9. In his forever home, Star realized that he was a winner each day, and yet he didn't win a blue ribbon. What makes Star a winner?
   a. Star now believes in himself and knows he is beautiful.
   b. Star knows he is special and valuable.
   c. Star knows he is loved, no matter what!

10. Which one of these makes you more valuable?
    a. Winning a ribbon or prize.
    b. Getting a good grade in school.
    c. My value is not determined by my success. I am always valuable.

Answer key: (1) A,B (2) A,C (3) B (4) A,B (5) B,C (6) A,B,C (7) A,C (8) A,B,C (9) A,B,C (10) C

Promising Puppy Vocabulary

Responsible Dog Owner: A person who cares for the needs of his dog, and is committed to that care throughout the pet's life. A responsible dog owner loves his dog and keeps him safe, healthy, and happy. He makes sure his dog is trained and well behaved in public. He also respects laws such as properly disposing of a dog's waste, and local leash laws.

Commitment: In the context of this story, commitment means that the dog's owner is loyal to his pet and will make sure his dog is well cared for, happy, and loved all the days of his life.

Dog Breeder: A person who raises dogs. A responsible breeder works to improve the breed and makes sure the pups, as well as the mother and father, are well cared for and loved. A responsible breeder will not let a puppy go to a new home when it's too young, or before it's had the proper vaccinations and socialization. A responsible breeder is willing to talk, answer questions, and is there for you and your puppy throughout its life.

Understanding: In the context of this story, understanding means that the dog owner should try at all times to comprehend (sympathize with) the thoughts and moods of his dog.

Praise: In the context of this story, praise means to express approval and admiration towards your dog. This is especially important while training your dog. Everyone can benefit from praise.

Love: Deep affection, fondness, tenderness. In the context of this story, love means that the dog owner shares a mutual affection, loyalty, and bond with his dog. This love is expressed in time spent together— playing, training, and caring for a dog's emotional and physical needs. UNCONDITIONAL LOVE SAYS, "I WILL LOVE YOU NO MATTER WHAT."

Veterinarian (vet): An animal doctor.

Caring: A caring person is one who is kind and shows concern for others. In the context of this story, a caring dog owner shows concern for his dog's needs, both physical and mental.

Inner Beauty: The inner qualities of a person that shine out, such as kindness, compassion, honesty, and loving others.

Self-Worth: A deep knowing that you are valuable as a person. Self worth is about who you are, not about what you do. God made us in his image and deeply loves us, therefore we are all valuable and worthy of love and respect. Understanding this builds a healthy sense of self worth.

Learn More About Star: Q & A

Q. What kind of dog breed is Star?

A. Star is a Cavalier King Charles Spaniel.

Q. How did the Cavalier King Charles Spaniel get their name?

A. For centuries, this breed was an inseparable companion to European nobility. King Charles II, who was very fond of the breed, gave them their name.

Q. How much does the Cavalier King Charles Spaniel weigh, and how tall are they?

A. They weigh between 13–18 pounds and are considered a "toy breed." They are 12-13 inches in height.

Q What colors does the Cavalier King Charles come in?

A. They come in four colors—Blenheim, Tricolor, Ruby, and Black and Tan.

Q. What color is Star?

A. Star is a Blenheim, which means he has rich chestnut markings on a pearly white background.

Q. What is the personality of the Cavalier King Charles Spaniel?

This breed is gentle, affectionate, active, elegant, and very friendly! They are also called, "Comforter Spaniels" and love being close to their family and sitting in their laps.

FUN FACT: Did you know that Cavalier King Charles Spaniel pups, like Star, are born with a pink nose? As they grow, the pigment turns black. Look back in chapter 1 and try to find the photos where Star's nose is pink.

PLEASE ADOPT, OR CHOOSE YOUR NEXT PUPPY FROM A CARING, RESPONSIBLE BREEDER.

Dog Care Items: Word Search

Positive affirmation: I am responsible.

Try to find the hidden words. Words can be down ↓ or from left to right →. Good luck!

```
G B N M O E O J Z M F M X N G
B X P N I B R U S H V S W S Z
L N T N J T U B M D O G T A G
G R O O M I N G S P R A Y A U
E W A T E R B O W L E Z N B J
T S X V R A T J A L I X L F T
O X L E A S H K C O L L A R O
W P W T R E A T S B D T G C O
X S D O G S H A M P O O F O T
S L M J B P B O O D G E G M H
G F O O D B O W L T F E V B B
R Z P P B H B J O C O A C Z R
O C S E J S X H K E O V H M U
X K N X M R M X W C R D C I G S
K Y H N W A S Z Q V H B E R H
```

Grooming Spray　　Dog Shampoo　　Toothbrush　　Water Bowl
Dog Food　　　　　Food Bowl　　　Collar　　　　Dog Tag
Treats　　　　　　Brush　　　　　Leash　　　　 Comb

Color the Dog Care Items

POSITIVE AFFIRMATION: I CARE FOR MY PET.

Word Search Answer Key

HELP THE DOG FIND HIS BONE!

POSITIVE AFFIRMATION: I AM HELPFUL.

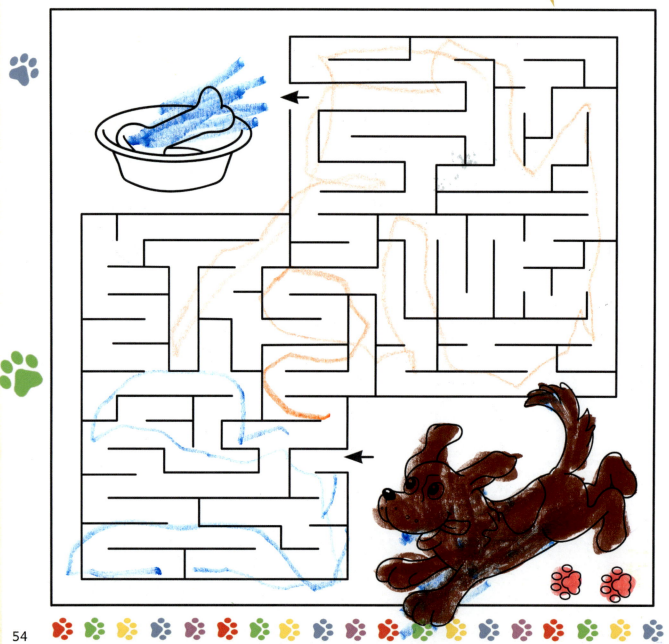

Coloring Page

Positive affirmation: I am loved!

A Promise to My Dog

Directions: Use the word bank below to find the word that best fits in each sentence. Fill in the blanks.

I, (write your name)_____ will do my best to be a responsible dog owner. I will spend (1)_____ with my dog, play with him or her often, and give my pet lots of love and (2)_____. I know that my pet needs clean (3)_____ to drink and good (4)_____ to eat each day in order to be happy and healthy. He also needs to be brushed and (5)_____ and regular exercise. My dog's health and (6)_____ are very important. He needs to see a (7)_____ for his vaccinations and check-ups. I will make sure he wears a (8)_____ and ID tag. I will keep training fun and reward him with lots of (9)_____ and (10)_____. If mistakes happen, I will be (11)_____ and (12)_____. I will be careful not to leave my dog alone for too long. I know that my (13)_____ will always love me, and I will always (14)_____ him in return. This is my promise to my dog.

Word Bank

affection	praise	kind	patient	gentle
food	treats	water	love	dog
bathed	time	veterinarian	collar	safety

Answer key: (1) time (2) affection (3) water (4) food (5) bathed (6) safety (7) veterinarian (8) collar (9) praise (10) treats (11) patient (12) kind (13) dog (14) love

"A Promise to My Dog" may be reproduced for classroom or individual use only. © 2020 Leila Grandemange

A Promise to Myself

Directions: Use the word bank below to find the word that best fits in the paragraph. Fill in the blanks.

I, (write your name)_____ will do my best to think good and (1)_____ thoughts about myself. I believe I am unique, beautiful, and (2)_____. There is no one better to be than (3)_____. I will remember that my worth does not depend on what others (4)_____ about me, or my accomplishments, or anything else. I will believe in myself and remember that my worth comes from (5)_____. And God will always (6)_____ me, even on my worst days. I will do my best to be a good, (7)_____, and caring person. When I mess up, I will (8)_____ myself and try better next time. When others (9)_____ ____, I will also forgive them and remember that nobody is (10)_____. When challenges come, I will use them to help me grow stronger. I (11)_____ in myself. I like who I am. I accept who I am. I will accept others and celebrate our (12)_____. Each day, I will do my (13)_____ to love myself and others unconditionally. This is my promise to myself.

Word Bank

love, kind, believe, God, patient, differences, forgive, mess up, perfect, think, myself, valuable, positive, best

Answer Key: (1) positive (2) valuable (3) myself (4) think (5) God (6) love (7) kind (8) forgive (9) mess up (10) perfect (11) believe (12) differences (13) best

"A Promise to Myself" may be reproduced for classroom or individual use only. © 2020 Leila Grandemange

50 Fabulous Positive Affirmations

Feel good about yourself. Say these daily affirmations as often as you like! You can photocopy this page and place it where you will see it often.

1. I am valuable.
2. God loves me.
3. I am unique.
4. I matter.
5. My words and feelings matter.
6. I am special.
7. I believe in myself.
8. I am beautiful inside and out.
9. I spread joy everywhere I go.
10. I like myself.
11. I am worthy of respect.
12. I have confidence when I speak.
13. I am strong and courageous.
14. I am a hard worker.
15. I take care of my body and mind.
16. I deserve to be loved.
17. I am a good friend.
18. I am a good listener.
19. I accept others for who they are.
20. I am respectful.
21. I am patient.
22. I am loving.
23. I am caring and kind.
24. I am forgiving.
25. I am generous.
26. It's okay not to be perfect.
27. God accepts me.
28. I am a good influence on others.
29. I learn from my mistakes.
30. I learn from challenges.
31. It's okay to make mistakes; I am human.
32. If I fall I will get back up.
33. Today is a brand new start!
34. I am excited about my abilities.
35. I am capable of great things!
36. I feel good about who I am.
37. I have faith in God.
38. Things will be okay.
39. I am thankful.
40. I am truthful.
41. I do what is right.
42. It's okay not to know everything.
43. I do my best each day.
44. I am proud of myself.
45. I stay calm.
46. I talk to God about my life.
47. I have a friend in Jesus.
48. I get better each day.
49. There is no one better to be than me.
50. I am enough!

Write your own positive affirmation: _____

My Favorite Affirmations

Write your favorite affirmations in the yellow stars.
You can photocopy this page and place it where you will see it often.

I AM A STAR

Online Resources for Kids & Parents

Caring for Pets: Resources for Kids

1. **A Puppy Contract for Kids:** www.Loveyourdog.com/contract
2. **How to Love Your Dog:** Interactive site for kids with dogs. www.Howtoloveyourdog.com
3. **The American Kennel Club Activities for Children:** www.Akc.org/public-education/
4. **The Dog Listener:** Safety Around Dogs Program (PDF) www.Images.akc.org/pdf/PBSAF2.pdf
5. **Family Paws Parent Education:** www.Familypaws.com/

Nurturing Self Worth: Parent Resources

6. **Kids Play and Create:** Kid approved self-esteem activities. www.Kidsplayandcreate.com/self-esteem-character-building-activities-for-kids/
7. **Children's Library Lady:** Self-esteem book list. Childrenslibrarylady.com/self-esteem-grid/
8. **Focus on the Family:** Leading Christian Parenting Website. www.Focusonthefamily.com/parenting/building-self-esteem-in-your-kids/
9. **Confident Body Confident Child:** www.Confidentbody.net/
10. **"I Am Special" with Grover:** www.Youtube.com/watch?v=Gms-Yk7mzv4

Heartfelt Thanks

To my precious family: Thank you for always believing in me and offering input and support throughout this project.

To my beloved dogs: Thank you for filling our home with happiness and lavishing us daily with unconditional love.

To my Heavenly Father: Thank you for loving me unconditionally, and showing me that I am infinitely valuable, no matter what!

To Parents and Educators

A review by Maryscott "Scotti" Glasgow, Ed.D

Star, A Promising Puppy by Leila Grandemange is so much more than a cute little book with lovely photos of a beautiful puppy. This poignant story is embedded with life lessons for potential pet owners, parents, educators, and children. The puppy's basic physical needs are being met. He is fed, has water, and is safe from harm. However, he is lacking friendship and acceptance causing his emotional needs not to be met. Therefore, his esteem cannot be formed and actualization cannot be realized according to Abraham Maslow's research. Luckily, the puppy finds a home where ALL his needs are met; therefore, his inner beauty and confidence are able to shine through.

Even though targeted for primary and elementary grades, these inspiring lessons can be adapted for children of all ages. Grandemange's rhyming text is easy to read and flows beautifully. At the end of her story she provides fun follow-up activities to help children learn more about dog care and also about living with the awareness that they are valuable and very much loved! *Star, A Promising Puppy* is already on my shelf. I recommend that it should be on a library shelf of every elementary classroom.

Maryscott "Scotti" Glasgow, Ed.D.
Former classroom teacher and college professor;
developer of digital math curriculum and
math facilitator for the Little Rock (AR) School District

About the Author

Leila Grandemange is the author of several charming books, an award-winning writer, and recipient of the AKC Responsible Dog Ownership Public Service Award. She participates in various dog sports, has bred and shown numerous AKC champions, and is recognized as an AKC Breeder of Merit.

Animals have always been a part of her life. Whether showing horses or dogs, cleaning stalls or caring for her pets, Leila grew up to appreciate the immense joy and responsibility of sharing life with animals. Today, Leila writes to inspire hope in daily life and to promote the responsible care of our furry friends!

Leila has a B.A. in Christian Education and has taught children from elementary through middle school. To learn more about Leila and her books or to subscribe to her blog, please visit **www.LeilaGrandemange.com.**

Children are a gift from above, entrusted to us like precious seeds. We water them with praise, patience, and love, and watch them grow into full bloom.

— Leila Grandemange

Thanks for reading the tale of Star!
Please add a short review on Amazon and let others know what you thought.

Made in the USA
Middletown, DE
29 December 2020